KEN

CREATE PERSONAL AFFIRMATIONS THAT EMPOWER YOU TO *show up* AND *shine*

LiveItForward.com

Affirm Yourself—Create Personal Affirmations that Empower You to Show
Up and Shine
Copyright © 2015 by Kent Julian

Published by Live It Forward LLC
Lawrenceville, GA

Printed in the Untied States of America

ISBN-13: 978-0-9777363-6-2

This book is available for quantity discounts for bulk purchases.

For additional information about Kent Julian and Live It Forward LLC,
visit us on the web at **www.liveitforward.com** or email us at
info@liveitforward.com.

Dedication

This book is dedicated to all the direct sales professionals and home-based business owners I am privileged to know. Your passion for pursuing freedom in the work and life you love inspires me!

Acknowledgements

Thank you to Jill Davis of JillDavisCoaching.com. I have learned so much from you about what it takes to succeed in direct sales. Thank you for your insight and friendship.

Thank you to Emily Chase Smith of ChaseSmithPress.com. Your editing skills make it look like I write "good" (smile). Whenever I'm in a conversation with another author, I recommend your services.

Thank you to Mary Kay Ash. Although I never met you, what I have learned from your books and organization has positively impacted me personally and professionally. You summed up the Live It Forward philosophy when you said: "God first. Family second. Business third."

Thank you to Dan Miller of 48Days.com. I am blessed to be living the life I'm living and doing the work I love. Without your coaching and influence, it would have never been possible. I am forever grateful.

Finally, thank you to the love of my life, Kathy. Not only are you an amazing spouse and my best friend, you're a great editor too (smile). I love doing life with you!

Kent Julian
June 2015

Contents

Why So Short?

Let's tackle the first question you're probably asking about this book. *Why is it so short?*

That's easy. As someone who has authored, co-authored, and contributed to nine non-fiction books including this one, I have written long and short books. In each case, there was a specific purpose regarding the book's length. For longer books, the primary purpose was to inform readers. For shorter books, the purpose was for readers to take action.

So...

THIS BOOK IS ABOUT TAKING ACTION! You don't need to wade through 50 to 75 pages of information before crafting your own personal affirmation statements. What you need to do is: TAKE ACTION.

What Are Affirmations?

Affirmations are powerful, positive statements you make to yourself. More specifically, they are powerful, positive statements you make to yourself:

➡ On a regular basis
➡ In the present tense
➡ To affirm what you believe about yourself and the life you want to live

Affirmations are *already, not yet* statements. They are powerful, positive statements you *already* believe to be true about yourself and your life, even though they often are *not yet* your reality. In other words, they are powerful, positive statements that shape your present and predict your future.

Ideally…

➡ You repeat your affirmations every day.
➡ Affirmations equip you to live it forward.
➡ Affirmations empower you to show up and shine in your most important life roles such as spouse, parent, business owner, and friend.

Bottom line, affirmations articulate the way you will live your best life no matter what circumstances or challenges you face.

Why Don't Affirmations Work?

If affirmations are so powerful, why don't they work?

In a word, most affirmations are "fake." More specifically, they are fake to you.

Most affirmations are promoted as copy-and-paste tools. Yet when other people create affirmations for you to copy-and-paste into your life, the affirmations have little impact on you because they are not authentic to you. They belong to someone else.

For affirmations to be powerful, you must create them. They must come from your DNA so they are authentic, personal, and heartfelt.

How to Make Affirmations Work for You?

How do you create your own affirmations? How do you make sure they come from your DNA and are not just a parroting of someone else's desires or reality?

Easy. You write them yourself.

"Wait a minute," you say to yourself. "Write my own *already, not yet* affirmations? Write personal, powerful statements that inspire me to live it forward in my most important life roles? That doesn't sound easy, it sounds hard!"

It is hard . . . unless you have a system designed to make it simple for you to connect with what you believe about yourself and the life you want to live. With that baseline, it's easy to craft your own powerful affirmations that resonate with you and turn what you already believe into your reality.

How to Create Your Personal Affirmations?

Each of the 30 affirmations in this book begins with an inspirational quote and then asks a direct question. The thoughts each question elicits in you is the secret sauce that will allow you to easily fashion a powerful, personal affirmation. The process is simple, yet deep.

There are several guidelines we will cover in the next few pages, but before we jump in, I want to give you an example of what I'm talking about—an authentic, personal, and heartfelt affirmation intricately tied to who you are and who you want to become.

The Affirmation Writing Process: A Personal Example from Kent

Quote: Do the best people in your life get the best from you?

Question: What can you do daily to guarantee your family gets your best instead of your leftovers?

Thoughts:

→ Put Kathy above everyone else in my life. Even above our children.

→ Put our children second.

→ Don't just say: "I love you" to my family, live "I love you."

→ Daily look for ways to serve Kathy and our children.

Personal Affirmation: I daily choose to live and serve in such a way that Kathy and our kids can look at me and say with pride, "That's my husband" and "That's my dad."

A Word About the Quotes in This Book

All the quotes in this book are mine. That's right, I own them (smile).

In all seriousness, the quotes in this book are personal to me, but I have no expectation that you will use them in your everyday life. In fact, if you do, I will be disappointed. Instead, these quotes will help you shape your own affirmations. Additionally, I hope the process of working through this book leads you to your own quotes. When this happens I'll have a big, toothy grin on my face because I will have done my job of helping you find your voice and create your own affirmations.

Before You Begin
(3 Important Guidelines)

Finally, before you begin, there are three important guidelines to keep in mind when writing personal affirmations.

First, write in **present tense**. Even though you will likely write *not yet* statements, write them as if they are *already* true. Use present tense phrases such as:

I am

I have

I _____ (articulate the action you "are" taking)

Second, use **positive phrases** instead of negative ones. For instance: *I am wise with money. I joyfully save 10 percent of everything I earn because I understand the power of compound interest. I also have a financial freedom jar that I gladly put additional money into every single day.*

Here is the same affirmation using negative phrases. Notice the difference: *I do not waste money on silly expenses. Instead, I work hard to save 10 percent of everything I make. I also have a financial freedom jar and scrape to put a little bit of extra money into it every day.*

The first statement focuses on the positive pursuit of being proactive. The second statement zeroes in on the challenges associated with taking action. The first statement inspires; the second statement deflates.

Third, tap into the power of the **Pareto Principle** (i.e. The 80/20 Rule). The Pareto Principle states that 20 percent of your efforts produce 80 percent of your results. Although this book contains 30 quotes and questions, you don't want to repeat 30 affirmations every day. That's way too many! Instead, use this book to develop 30 potential affirmations and pick 6-10 that inspire you the most. These 6-10 affirmations are your 20 percent that will empower you to achieve 80 percent of your results and allow you to live it forward into your dream reality.

AFFIRM YOURSELF

Creating Personal Affirmations That Empower You to Show Up and Shine

Quote #1:

Show Up and Shine

Every day you are faced with a choice.
Check out and whine or
SHOW UP AND SHINE.
Do something today to make it a
#showupandshine day!

Affirm Yourself

Question: What can you do to Show Up and Shine every day in every way?

Thoughts: _____

_____

_____

_____

_____

_____

_____

_____

_____

Personal Affirmation: _____

_____

_____

_____

Quote #2:

Thankfulness

Successful people focus on
thankfulness
instead of entitlement.

Affirm Yourself

Question: How can you make thankfulness pour out of you like a spring?

Thoughts: _____

_____

_____

_____

_____

_____

_____

_____

_____

Personal Affirmation: _____

_____

_____

_____

_____

Quote #3:

Family

Do the best people in your life
get the best from you?

Affirm Yourself

Question: What can you do daily to guarantee your family gets your best instead of your leftovers?

Thoughts: _____

_____

_____

_____

_____

_____

_____

_____

_____

Personal Affirmation: _____

_____

_____

_____

Quote #4:

Goals

The real power of a goal is not found in the process of setting it.
The real power of a goal is found in the process of achieving it.

Affirm Yourself

Question: Goals are achieved one step at a time. How can you take at least one step every day to achieve your goals?

Thoughts: _____

_____

_____

_____

_____

_____

_____

_____

_____

Personal Affirmation: _____

_____

_____

_____

_____

Quote #5:

Success

Becoming successful is pretty simple.

BUT IT'S NOT EASY.

Affirm Yourself

Question: What will help you achieve success
no matter how hard it is or how long it takes?

Thoughts: _____

_____

_____

_____

_____

_____

_____

_____

_____

Personal Affirmation: _____

_____

_____

_____

_____

Quote #6:

Destiny

Direction determines destiny.
The moment you change your
direction, you change your destiny.

Affirm Yourself

Question: How do you take charge of your direction?

Thoughts: _____

_____

_____

_____

_____

_____

_____

_____

_____

_____

Personal Affirmation: _____

_____

_____

_____

Positivity

Positivity attracts and builds up.

Negativity repels and tears down.

Affirm Yourself

Question: What will you do to become one of the most realistically positive people on the planet?

Thoughts: _____

_____

_____

_____

_____

_____

_____

_____

_____

Personal Affirmation: _____

_____

_____

_____

_____

Quote #8:

Fear

Some people say they are
afraid of failure.
Others say they are afraid of success.
The truth is most people are afraid of
their hard work not paying off.

Affirm Yourself

Question: How can you overcome your fear of your hard work not paying off?

Thoughts: _____

_____

_____

_____

_____

_____

_____

_____

_____

_____

Personal Affirmation: _____

_____

_____

_____

_____

Quote #9:

Persistence

Stick-to-it-tiveness is your greatest

competitive advantage.

It instantly puts you in the

top 10 percent.

Affirm Yourself

Question: What will you do to stay committed to your dream reality even when it's overwhelmingly difficult?

Thoughts: _____

_____

_____

_____

_____

_____

_____

_____

_____

_____

Personal Affirmation: _____

_____

_____

_____

Quote #10:

Excuses

Excuses and success don't play well together in the same sandbox.

Affirm Yourself

Question: What will you do to kick excuses out of your sandbox once and for all?

Thoughts: _____

_____

_____

_____

_____

_____

_____

_____

_____

Personal Affirmation: _____

_____

_____

_____

Quote #11:

Greatness

Don't let acceptable be acceptable.

GO FOR GREAT!

Affirm Yourself

Question: What actions can you take to be great?

Thoughts: _____

_____

_____

_____

_____

_____

_____

_____

_____

_____

Personal Affirmation: _____

_____

_____

_____

_____

Quote #12:

Failure

Failure turns into success the moment you LEARN and GROW from it.

Affirm Yourself

Question: How can you learn and grow from every failure you face?

Thoughts: _____

_____

_____

_____

_____

_____

_____

_____

_____

_____

Personal Affirmation: _____

_____

_____

_____

Obstacles

Removing obstacles is progress.

Affirm Yourself

Question: How will you remove obstacles that present themselves to you?

Thoughts: _____

_____

_____

_____

_____

_____

_____

_____

_____

Personal Affirmation: _____

_____

_____

_____

Quote #14:

Luck

Good luck is a byproduct of taking more positive steps than other people.

Affirm Yourself

Question: How can you create more "good luck" in your life?

Thoughts: _____

_____

_____

_____

_____

_____

_____

_____

_____

Personal Affirmation: _____

_____

_____

_____

Your Past

Don't stare in the rearview mirror.
Glance long enough to learn from your
past and then keep your gaze
on your horizon.
Live It Forward!

Affirm Yourself

Question: What will you do to keep your gaze on your horizon instead of in your rearview mirror?

Thoughts: _____

_____

_____

_____

_____

_____

_____

_____

_____

Personal Affirmation: _____

_____

_____

_____

Quote #16:

Great Ideas

Great ideas are worthless.
The execution of great ideas is where
you'll find the real value.

Affirm Yourself

Question: How will you act on your great ideas?

Thoughts: _____

_____

_____

_____

_____

_____

_____

_____

_____

_____

_____

Personal Affirmation: _____

_____

_____

_____

_____

Quote #17:

Money

You don't make money.

You earn it.

Affirm Yourself

Question: How will you earn money?

Thoughts: _____

_____

_____

_____

_____

_____

_____

_____

_____

Personal Affirmation: _____

_____

_____

_____

_____

Quote #18:

Self-Image

Until you begin to see
who you could be,
you will never take steps to
become all you can be.

Affirm Yourself

Question: What daily habits will you practice to cultivate a healthy self-image?

Thoughts: _____

_____

_____

_____

_____

_____

_____

_____

_____

Personal Affirmation: _____

_____

_____

_____

_____

Choices

A choice is more than a decision.

A choice requires action.

Affirm Yourself

Question: How will you choose to take action on your decisions?

Thoughts: _____

_____

_____

_____

_____

_____

_____

_____

Personal Affirmation: _____

_____

_____

_____

Quote #20:

Coaching

Great leaders COACH UP
instead of talk down.

Affirm Yourself

Question: How will you coach your team up?

Thoughts: _____

_____

_____

_____

_____

_____

_____

_____

_____

_____

_____

Personal Affirmation: _____

_____

_____

_____

_____

Quote #21:

Happiness

**Happiness is not a character trait;
it's a choice.**

Affirm Yourself

Question: How will you choose happiness?

Thoughts: _____

_____

_____

_____

_____

_____

_____

_____

_____

_____

Personal Affirmation: _____

_____

_____

_____

Quote #22:

Stretching Yourself

Often the best action you can
take is also the most uncomfortable
action you can take.

Affirm Yourself

Question: How can you become more com-
fortable with being uncomfortable?

Thoughts: _____

_____

_____

_____

_____

_____

_____

_____

_____

_____

Personal Affirmation: _____

_____

_____

_____

_____

Quote #23:

Drama

Run away from DRAMA so you can run towards your DREAMS.

Affirm Yourself

Question: How will you stay away from drama?

Thoughts: _____

_____

_____

_____

_____

_____

_____

_____

_____

Personal Affirmation: _____

_____

_____

_____

_____

Decision Making

Run AT problems and decisions
instead of running away from them.

Affirm Yourself

Question: What will you do to proactively make decisions and solve problems?

Thoughts: _____

_____

_____

_____

_____

_____

_____

_____

_____

Personal Affirmation: _____

_____

_____

_____

Quote #25:

Listening

The opposite of talking is not
waiting to speak.
The opposite of talking is
engaged listening.

Affirm Yourself

Question: How will you become a more engaged listener?

Thoughts: _____

_____

_____

_____

_____

_____

_____

_____

_____

Personal Affirmation: _____

_____

_____

_____

_____

Quote #26:

Leadership

Want to lead others?
Successfully lead yourself first.

Affirm Yourself

Question: How will you be a leader others look up to and follow?

Thoughts: _____

_____

_____

_____

_____

_____

_____

_____

_____

Personal Affirmation: _____

_____

_____

_____

Quote #27:

Personal Development

Success principles are

like suntan lotion.

They only work if you rub them in.

Affirm Yourself

Question: What will you do to invest in your personal and professional development every day?

Thoughts: _____

_____

_____

_____

_____

_____

_____

_____

_____

_____

Personal Affirmation: _____

_____

_____

_____

_____

Quote #28:

Ambition

Talent's good . . . but it will never
take you as far as ambition.

Affirm Yourself

Question: What will you do to become a more ambitious person?

Thoughts: _____

_____

_____

_____

_____

_____

_____

_____

_____

Personal Affirmation: _____

_____

_____

_____

Quote #29:

Action

What you believe is evidenced by the STEPS you take, not by the WORDS you say.

Affirm Yourself

Question: How will you take action on what you say you believe?

Thoughts: _____

_____

_____

_____

_____

_____

_____

_____

_____

_____

Personal Affirmation: _____

_____

_____

_____

Quote #30:

Live It Forward

Move towards your dream reality
one step at a time, one day at
a time. Don't just live it up or
live for the moment . . .
LIVE IT FORWARD!

Affirm Yourself

Question: How will you live it forward instead of just living it up or living for the moment?

Thoughts: _____

_____

_____

_____

_____

_____

_____

_____

_____

Personal Affirmation: _____

_____

_____

_____

BONUS TIME!
(Additional Quotes)

If you love quotes and feel like the previous 30 just weren't enough, here are a few more as an added-value bonus for you. Enjoy!

In a prizefight between planning and taking action, taking action always wins.

Success is a process, not a place. Set meaningful goals and enjoy the process of success.

Worry focuses on the bad that might happen. Gratitude focuses on the good that has happened. Choose gratitude!

Losers blame others and make excuses. Winners share credit and give reasons.

Good leaders focus on results. Great leaders focus on empowering their team and let results take care of themselves.

Practice the art of praising people towards success.

The best leaders treat people the best.

Even mundane tasks are enjoyable when they are connected to work you love.

Never follow directions from someone who hasn't been where you want to go.

Frankness from a close friend is better than flattery from a distant follower.

Today is a special gift waiting to be unwrapped. Jump out of bed, tear it open, and start playing right away.

Turn failure into fertilizer instead of your final resting place.

Want to be amazing? Ask yourself what you would do at this moment to be amazing and do that.

Success isn't easy. It's earned.

Live It Forward

and earn   with Kent Julian

Kent Julian is founder and president of Live It Forward LLC (liveitforward.com), which inspires and equips direct sales professionals and home-based business owners to SHOW UP AND SHINE in life and business. He is a highly sought-after speaker and coach who annually presents in 40-50 venues to 40,000-50,000 high achievers on topics such as Success Strategies for Direct Sales Professionals, Unleashing High Potential Leaders, and Direction Determines Destiny.

Kent strongly believes the reason people fall short in their direct sales and home-based businesses isn't due to a lack of passion or commitment, but it's because they treat their business like a hobby. Through live events, online training, and coaching programs, Kent equips direct sales professionals and home-based business owners with the mindset and skills necessary for achieving ultimate success in both life and business.

For more information or to schedule Kent to speak at your next event, visit **liveitforward.com** or email **info@liveit forward.com**.